Books by Anthony Hecht

POETRY

The Transparent Man   1990
Collected Earlier Poems   1990
The Venetian Vespers   1979
Millions of Strange Shadows   1977
The Hard Hours   1967
A Summoning of Stones   1954

TRANSLATION

Aeschylus's Seven Against Thebes   1973
(WITH HELEN BACON)

ESSAYS

Obbligati   1986

THE TRANSPARENT MAN

THE TRANSPARENT MAN

POEMS BY

ANTHONY HECHT

Alfred A. Knopf   *New York*   1990

THIS IS A BORZOI BOOK
PUBLISHED BY ALFRED A. KNOPF, INC.

The following poems were originally published as indicated:

Poem Without Anybody, The Kenyon Review, Vol. II, #4, Fall 1980
Meditation, Vogue, November 1981
Devotions of a Painter, New Statesman, June 25, 1982
The Book of Yolek, New Statesman, June 25, 1982
The Transparent Man, New England Review, Winter 1980
A Love For Four Voices, Poetry, April, 1981
Murmur, The New Yorker, March 16, 1981
Anthem, Poetry, October 1982
Antapodosis, The Atlantic, November 1982
Humoresque, The Paris Review, Summer/Fall 1986
Envoi, The Yale Review, Vol. 76, #1, Autumn 1987
A Bountiful Harvest, Washington Post Book World, November 28, 1982
Terms, The New Yorker, April 22, 1985
Eclogue, The Sewanee Review, Summer 1989
Naming the Animals, The New York Review of Books, August 17, 1989

I am deeply grateful for substantial help and generous encouragement to the
Ruth Lilly Foundation, the Aiken Taylor Fund of The Sewanee Review, The
National Endowment for The Arts, and to the following publications where
some of these poems first appeared: The New Yorker, The New York Review of
Books, The New Statesman, The New England Review, The Atlantic Monthly,
Vogue, Poetry, The Paris Review, The Kenyon Review, The Sewanee Review, and
The Yale Review.

For HELEN *and* *for* EVAN

CONTENTS

I

II

III

IV

V

I

CURRICULUM VITAE

As though it were reluctant to be day,
　　Morning deploys a scale
　　Of rarities in gray,
And winter settles down in its chain-mail,

Victorious over legions of gold and red.
　　The smokey souls of stones,
　　Blunt pencillings of lead,
Pare down the world to glintless monotones

Of graveyard weather, vapors of a fen
　　We reckon through our pores.
　　Save for the garbage men,
Our children are the first ones out of doors.

Book-bagged and padded out, at mouth and nose
　　They manufacture ghosts,
　　George Washington's and Poe's,
Banquo's, the Union and Confederate hosts',

And are themselves the ghosts, file cabinet gray,
　　Of some departed us,
　　Signing our lives away
On ferned and parslied windows of a bus.

RIDDLES

And the Spirit of God moved upon
the face of the waters.

Where the wind listeth, there the sailboats list,
    Water is touched with a light case of hives
Or wandering gooseflesh. The strange power and gist
    Of whatever it is that animates our lives

Scrawls with a lavish hand its signature
    Of ripples gathered into folds and pleats
As indecipherable, chiselled, pure,
    And everlasting as the name of Keats.

The surface wrinkles in spirit-shapes that sprint
    Like small rapids or frightened schools of fish;
They blot out images of cloud, the print
    Of passing hulls, obeying something's wish.

These vagrant hieroglyphs, now here, now there,
    In which the fate of everything lies writ
By the invisible majesty of air,
    Prove we are one and all illiterate,

And should be asking: "What do they portend?"
    Other, please God, than those fiery words for coins
That signified to Belshazzar the end
    Of all his hopes and the issue of his loins.

CHORUS FROM OEDIPUS AT COLONOS

What is unwisdom but the lusting after
Longevity: to be old and full of days!
For the vast and unremitting tide of years
Casts up to view more sorrowful things than joyful;
And as for pleasures, once beyond our prime,
They all drift out of reach, they are washed away.
And the same gaunt bailiff calls upon us all,
Summoning into Darkness, to those wards
Where is no music, dance, or marriage hymn
That soothes or gladdens. To the tenements of Death.

Not to be born is, past all yearning, best.
And second best is, having seen the light,
To return at once to deep oblivion.
When youth has gone, and the baseless dreams of youth,
What misery does not then jostle man's elbow,
Join him as a companion, share his bread?
Betrayal, envy, calumny and bloodshed
Move in on him, and finally Old Age—
Infirm, despised Old Age—joins in his ruin,
The crowning taunt of his indignities.

So is it with that man, not just with me.
He seems like a frail jetty facing North
Whose pilings the waves batter from all quarters;
From where the sun comes up, from where it sets,
From freezing boreal regions, from below,
A whole winter of miseries now assails him,
Thrashes his sides and breaks over his head.

TERMS

For Derek Walcott

Holidays, books and lives draw to their close,
The curtain rings down on some theater piece,
The brass, string, and percussion sections close
In on their tonic and concordant close
When all loose ends infallibly are tied
Into baroque or plain completion. Close
Your eyes, and a childhood landscape wades in close
With delicate birch to supplant the frank disgrace
Of our littoral, littered world, as painters grace
A woman's grief, a beggar's bowl, with close
Clear scrutiny until a world has grown
Out of Rembrandt's pain and a narrow ghetto's groan.

Open your eyes. A body of water has grown
Obsidian, slick and ballroom smooth. Look close,
And, through a wind's light pucker, mark full-grown
Migrations of clouds, to which small fish have grown
Accustomed, which they inhabit, all of a piece
With their rock-bottom skies. And now the grown
Wind-wrinkles, the mackerel heavens, with their ingrown
Pisces and constellated summertide
Calm for an instant, arresting the whole tide
Of time, like ants in amber, momently grown
Changeless and still as painting, fluttering grace
Notes that are held in mind by an act of grace.

The young are full of an astonishing grace,
Soft-eyed, trustful and lithe till they have grown
Aware of being admired for their grace,
Whereupon they go through some fall from grace,
An aging that reminds us of our close.
The skater's tilt, the contemplator's grace
Are both a selflessness, evincing grace
In agile tension as well as mastered peace,

In a poise of speed or stillness. But our last peace,
Stone-capped, dark-rooted, engraved and void of grace,
Beds down in rain and rubble, and eventide
Sees us unsinewed, our last lank strands untied.

What do those distant thunderheads betide?
Nothing to do with us. Not our disgrace
That the raped corpse of a fourteen-year-old, tied
With friction tape, is found in a ditch, and a tide
Of violent crime breaks out. Yet the world grown
Wrathful, corrupt, once loosed a true floodtide
That inched inside the wards where the frail are tied
To their beds, invaded attics, climbed to disclose
Sharks in the nurseries, eels on the floors, to close
Over lives and cries and herds, and on that tide,
Which splintered barn, cottage and city piece-
Meal, one sole family rode the world to peace.

Think of the glittering morning when God's peace
Flooded the heavens as it withdrew the tide:
Sweet grasses, endless fields of such rich peace
That for long after, when men dreamed of peace,
It seemed a place where beast and human grace
A pastoral landscape, a Virgilian peace,
Or scene such as Mantegna's masterpiece
Of kneeling shepherds. But that dream has grown
Threadbare, improbable, and our paupers groan
While "stockpiled warheads guarantee our peace,"
And troops, red-handed, muscle in for the close.
Ours is a wound that bleeds and will not close.

Long since we had been cautioned: "Until he close
His eyes forever, mildly and in peace,
Call no man happy." The stain of our disgrace
Grows ominously, a malign, ingrown
Melanoma, softly spreading its dark tide.

DEVOTIONS OF A PAINTER

Cool sinuosities, waved banners of light,
Unfurl, remesh, and round upon themselves
In a continuing turmoil of benign
Cross-purposes, effortlessly as fish,
On the dark underside of the foot-bridge,
Cast upward against pewter-weathered planks.
Weeds flatten with the current. Dragonflies
Poise like blue needles, steady in mid-air,
For some decisive, swift inoculation.
The world repeats itself in ragged swatches
Among the lily-pads, but understated,
When observed from this selected vantage point,
A human height above the water-level,
As the shore shelves heavily over its reflection,
Its timid, leaf-strewn comment on itself.
It's midday in midsummer. Pitiless heat.
Not so much air in motion as to flutter
The frail, bright onion tissue of a poppy.
I am an elderly man in a straw hat
Who has set himself the task of praising God
For all this welter by setting out my paints
And getting as much truth as can be managed
Onto a small flat canvas. Constable
Claimed he had never seen anything ugly,
And would have known each crushed jewel in the pigments
Of these oily golds and greens, enamelled browns
That recall the glittering eyes and backs of frogs.
The sun dispenses its immense loose change,
Squandered on blossoms, ripples, mud, wet stones.
I am enamored of the pale chalk dust
Of the moth's wing, and the dark moldering gold
Of rust, the corrupted treasures of this world.
Against the Gospel let my brush declare:
"These are the anaglyphs and gleams of love."

DESTINATIONS

*The harvest is past, the summer is
ended, and we are not saved.*   JEREMIAH

The children having grown up and moved away,
One day she announced in brisk and scathing terms
That since for lo, as she said, these many years
She had thanklessly worked her fingers to the bone,
Always put him and the children first and foremost,
(A point he thought perhaps disputable)
She had had it up to here, and would be leaving
The following day, would send him an address
To which her belongings could be forwarded
And to which the monthly payments could be sent.
He could see her point. It was only tit for tat.
After all the years when the monthly pains were hers
They now were to be his. True to her word,
Which she commanded him to mark, she packed
And left, and took up shifting residence,
First with a barber, then with a state trooper:
From the scissors of severance to the leather holster
Of the well-slung groin—the six-pack, six-gun weapon
Of death and generation. He could see the point.
In these years of inflation ways and means
Had become meaner and more chancy ways
Of getting along. Economy itself
Urged perfect strangers to bed down together
Simply to make ends meet, and so ends met.
Rather to his surprise, his first reaction
Was a keen sense of relief and liberation.
It seemed that, thinking of her, he could recall
Only a catalogue of pettiness,
Selfishness, spite, a niggling litany
Of minor acrimony, punctuated
By outbursts of hysteria and violence.
Now there was peace, the balm of Gilead,
At least at first. Slowly it dawned upon him
That she had no incentive to remarry,

9

Since, by remaining single and shacking up,
She would enjoy two sources of income.
In the house of her deferred and mortgaged dreams
Two lived as cheaply as one, if both had funds.
He thought about this off and on for years
As he went on subsidizing her betrayal
In meek obedience to the court decree,
And watered the flowers by his chain-link fence
Beside the railroad tracks. In his back yard
He kept petunias in a wooden tub
Inside the white-washed tire of a tractor trailer,
And his kitchen steps of loose, unpainted boards
Afforded him an unimpeded view
Of the webbed laundry lines of all his neighbors,
Rusted petroleum tins, the buckled wheels
Of abandoned baby-carriages, and the black-
Sooted I-beams and girders of a bridge
Between two walls of rusticated stonework
Through which the six-fifteen conveyed the lucky
And favored to superior destinies.
Where did they go, these fortunates? He'd seen
Blonde, leggy girls pouting invitingly
In low-cut blouses on TV commercials,
And thought about encountering such a one
In a drugstore or supermarket. She
Would smile (according to his dream scenario)
And come straight home with him as if by instinct.
But in the end, he knew, this would be foreplay
To the main event when she'd take him to the cleaners.

ECLOGUE OF THE SHEPHERD AND THE TOWNIE

SHEPHERD

Not the blue-fountained Florida hotel,
Bell-capped, bellevued, straight-jacketed and decked
With chromium palms and a fromage of moon,
Not goodnight chocolates, nor the soothing slide
Of huîtres and sentinel straight-up martinis,
Neither the yacht heraldic nor the stretch
Limos and pants, Swiss banks or Alpine stocks
Shall solace you, or quiet the long pain
Of cold ancestral disinheritance,
Severing your friendly commerce with the beasts,
Gone, lapsed, and cancelled, rendered obsolete
As the gonfalon of Bessarabia,
The shawm, the jitney, the equestrian order,
The dark daguerreotypes of Paradise.

TOWNIE

No humble folding cot, no steaming sty
Or sheep-dipped meadow now shall dignify
Your brute and sordid commerce with the beasts,
Scotch your flea-bitten bitterness or down
The voice that keeps repeating, "Up your *Ars
Poetica*, your earliest diapered dream
Of the long-gone Odd Fellows amity
Of bunny and scorpion, the *entente cordiale*
Of lamb and lion, the old nursery fraud
And droll Aesopic zoo in which the chatter
Of chimp and chaffinch, manticore and mouse,
Diverts us from all thought of entrecôtes,
Prime ribs and rashers, filets mignonnettes,
Provided for the paired pythons and jackals,
Off to their catered second honeymoons
On Noah's forty-day excursion cruise."

SHEPHERD

Call it, if this should please you, but a dream,
A bald, long-standing lie and mockery,
Yet it deserves better than your contempt.
Think also of that interstellar darkness,
Silence and desolation from which the Tempter,
Like a space capsule exiled into orbit,
Looks down on our green cabinet of peace,
A place classless and weaponless, without
Envy or fossil fuel or architecture.
Think of him as at dawn he views a snail
Traveling with blind caution up the spine
Of a frond asway with its little inching weight
In windless nods that deepen with assent
Till the ambler at last comes back to earth,
Leaving his route, as on the boughs of heaven,
Traced with a silver scrawl. The morning mist
Haunts all about that action till the sun
Makes of it a small glory, and the dew
Holds the whole scale of rainbow, the accord
Of stars and waters, luminously viewed
At the same time by water-walking spiders
That dimple a surface with their passages.
In the lewd Viennese catalogue of dreams
It's one of the few to speak of without shame.

TOWNIE

It is the dream of a shepherd king or child,
And is without all blemish except one:
That it supposes all virtue to stem
From pure simplicity. But many cures
Of body and of spirit are the fruit
Of cultivated thought. Kindness itself
Depends on what we call consideration.
Your fear of corruption is a fear of thought,

Therefore you would be thoughtless. Think again.
Consider the perfect hexagrams of snow,
Those broadcast emblems of divinity,
That prove in their unduplicable shapes
Insights of Thales and Pythagoras.
If you must dream, dream of the ratio
Of Nine to Six to Four Palladio used
To shape those rooms and chapels where the soul
Imagines itself blessed, and finds its peace
Even in chambers of the *Malcontenta*,
Those just proportions we hypostatize
Not as flat prairies but the City of God.

MEDITATION

For William Alfred

Quatrocento put in paint,
On backgrounds for a God or Saint,
Gardens where the soul's at ease;
Where everything that meets the eye
Flowers and grass and cloudless sky
Resemble forms that are, or seem
When sleepers wake and yet still dream,
And when it's vanished still declare,
With only bed and bedstead there,
That Heavens had opened.

I

The orchestra tunes up, each instrument
In lunatic monologue putting on its airs,
Oblivious, haughty, full of self-regard.
The flute fingers its priceless strand of pearls,
Nasal disdain is eructed by the horn,
The strings let drop thin overtones of malice,
Inchoate, like the dense garbling of voices
At a cocktail party, which the ear sorts out
By alert exclusions, keen selectivities.
A five-way conversation, at its start
Smooth and intelligible as a Brahms quintet,
Disintegrates after one's third martini
To dull orchestral nonsense, the jumbled fragments
Of domestic friction in a foreign tongue,
Accompanied by a private sense of panic:
This surely must be how old age arrives,
Quite unannounced, when suddenly one fine day
Some trusted faculty has gone forever.

II

After the closing of cathedral doors,
After the last soft footfall fades away,
There still remain artesian, grottoed sounds
Below the threshold of the audible,
The infinite, unspent reverberations
Of the prayers, coughs, whispers and *amens* of the day,
Afloat upon the marble surfaces.
They continue forever. Nothing is ever lost.
So the sounds of children, enriched, magnified,
Cross-fertilized by the contours of a tunnel,
Promote their little statures for a moment
Of resonance to authority and notice,
A fleeting, bold celebrity that rounds
In perfect circles to attentive shores,
Returning now in still enlarging arcs
To which there is no end. Whirled without end.

III

This perfect company is here engaged
In what is called a sacred conversation.
A seat has been provided for the lady
With her undiapered child in a bright loggia
Floored with *antico verde* and alabaster
Which are cool and pleasing to the feet of saints
Who stand at either side. It is eight o'clock
On a sunny April morning, and there is much here
Worthy of observation. First of all,
No one in all the group seems to be speaking.
The Baptist, in a rude garment of hides,
Vaguely unkempt, is looking straight at the viewer
With serious interest, patient and unblinking.

Across from him, relaxed but powerful,
Stands St. Sebastian, who is neither a ruse
To get a young male nude with classic torso
Into an obviously religious painting,
Nor one who suffers his target martyrdom
Languidly or with a masochist's satisfaction.
He experiences a kind of acupuncture
That in its blessedness has set him free
To attend to everything except himself.
Jerome and Francis, the one in his red hat,
The other tonsured, both of them utterly silent,
Cast their eyes downward as in deep reflection.
Perched on a marble dais below the lady
A small seraphic consort of viols and lutes
Prepares to play or actually is playing.
They exhibit furrowed, child-like concentration.
A landscape of extraordinary beauty
Leads out behind the personages to where
A shepherd tends his flock. Far off a ship
Sets sail for the world of commerce. Travelers
Kneel at a wayside shrine near a stone wall.
Game-birds or song-birds strut or take the air
In gliding vectors among cypress spires
By contoured vineyards or groves of olive trees.
A belfry crowns a little knoll behind which
The world recedes into a cobalt blue
Horizon of remote, fine mountain peaks.

    The company, though they have turned their backs
To all of this, are aware of everything.
Beneath their words, but audible, the silver
Liquidities of stream and song-bird fall
In cleansing passages, and the water-wheel
Turns out its measured, periodic creak.
They hear the coughs, the raised voices of children
Joyful in the dark tunnel, everything.
Observe with care their tranquil pensiveness.

They hear all the petitions, all the cries
Reverberating over marble floors,
Floating above still water in dark wells.
All the world's woes, all the world's woven woes,
The warp of ages, they hear and understand,
To which is added a final bitterness:
That their own torments, deaths, renunciations,
Made in the name of love, have served as warrant,
Serve to this very morning as fresh warrant
For the infliction of new atrocities.
All this they know. Nothing is ever lost.
It is the condition of their blessedness
To hear and recall the recurrent cries of pain
And parse them into a discourse that consorts
In strange agreement with the viols and lutes,
Which, with the water and the meadow bells,
And every gathered voice, every *amen*,
Join to compose the sacred conversation.

II

SEE NAPLES AND DIE

*It is better to say, "I'm suffering," than
to say, "This landscape is ugly."* SIMONE WEIL

I

I can at last consider those events
Almost without emotion, a circumstance
That for many years I'd scarcely have believed.
We forget much, of course, and, along with facts,
Our strong emotions, of pleasure and of pain,
Fade into stark insensibility.
For which, perhaps, it need be said, thank God.
So I can read from my journal of that time
As if it were written by a total stranger.
Here is a sunny day in April, the air
Cool as spring water to breathe, but the sun warm.
We are seated under a trellised roof of vines,
Light-laced and freaked with grape-leaf silhouettes
That romp and buck across the tablecloth,
Flicker and slide on the white porcelain.
The air is scented with fresh rosemary,
Boxwood and lemon and a light perfume
From fields of wild-flowers far beyond our sight.
The cheap knives blind us. In the poet's words,
It is almost time for lunch. And the *padrone*
Invites us into blackness the more pronounced
For the brilliance of out-doors. Slowly our eyes
Make out his pyramids of delicacies—
The Celtic coils and curves of primrose shrimp,
A speckled gleam of opalescent squid,
The mussel's pearl-blue niches, as unearthly
As Brazilian butterflies, and the grey turbot,
Like a Picasso lady with both eyes
On one side of her face. We are invited
To choose our fare from this august display
Which serves as menu, and we return once more
To the sunshine, to the fritillary light

And shadow of our table where carafes
Of citrine wine glow with unstable gems,
Prison the sun like genie in their holds,
Enshrine their luminous spirits.
                                    There, before us,
The greatest amphitheater in the world:
Naples and its Bay. We have begun
Our holiday, Martha and I, in rustic splendor.
I look at her with love (was it with love?)
As a breeze takes casual liberties with her hair,
And set it down that evening in the hotel
(Where I make my journal entries after dinner)
That everything we saw this afternoon
After our splendid lunch with its noble view—
The jets of water, Diana in porphyry,
Callipygian, broad-bottomed Venus,
Whole groves of lemons, the packed grenadine pearls
Of pomegranate seeds, olive trees, urns,
All fired and flood-lit by this southern sun—
Bespoke an unassailable happiness.
And so it was. Or so I thought it was.
I believe that on that height I was truly happy,
Though I know less and less as time goes on
About what happiness is, unless it's what
Folk-wisdom celebrates as ignorance.
Dante says that the worst of all torments
Is to remember happiness once it's passed.
I am too numb to know whether he's right.

I I

Over the froth-white cowls of our morning coffee
I read to Martha from a battered guide-book
Which quotes a seventeenth-century diarist,
Candid and down-to-earth, on Naples' whores.
The city, he declared, proudly maintained

A corps of thirty-thousand registered sinners,
Taxed and inspected, issued licenses
For the custom of their bodies. One may assume
Their number, and the revenues of the state,
Must have compounded since those early days.
There were accounts, as well, of female beggars
With doped and rented children, and a rich trade
In pathos by assorted mendicants.
Baedeker, who is knowing in these matters,
Warns travelers against misguided kindness:
The importunate should be rebuffed with *niente*,
He firmly advises, and goes on to say
That poverty is a feature of the landscape.
Perhaps this strong fiduciary theme
Prompted attention to our own resources.
A six- or seven-year-old good-looking urchin
Had posted himself each day across the street
From our hotel, and from this vantage point
He offered tourists good black-market rates
Of currency exchange. I fell for this
For what, I suppose, are all the usual reasons.
There was first of all the charming oddity
Of a child-financier plying his trade
With such bright confidence. There was my pride,
The standard, anxious pride of every tourist,
Of wishing to exhibit worldly cunning
And not be subject to official rates.
And there was finally the curious lure
Of doing something questionably legal,
Which I could have no chance to do at home.
So I let the boy guide me through dark back alleys
To a small, grim, unprepossessing square,
Festooned with drying sheets and undergarments
Strung like blank banners high above our heads,
The ensigns of our nameless, furtive business.
He motioned me to wait, and disappeared.
There were two men across the square from me,

Conspicuous, vaguely thuggish, badly dressed,
In lively discourse, paying me no notice,
But filling me with a mild apprehension.
I could hear the whines of children, the louder wails
Of ambulances on their urgent missions
Somewhere far off, claiming their right of way.
The area smelled of garlic, soap, and urine.
And then young Ercole made his appearance.
He introduced himself. He was short, dark,
Athletic, with an air of insolence.
He was neatly dressed with very expensive shoes
In which he evidently took some pride,
A complex wrist-watch boasting several dials,
And delicate hands decked with a dazzle of rings.
Pride, as it seems, was governing us both.
I felt distinctly uncertain of myself
But saw no way before me to withdraw.
I noticed that as our talk got underway
The men across the square had ceased conversing
And were giving us their full consideration,
Which, given the cautious nature of our dealings,
Was far from reassuring. But Ercole,
Who seemed aware that we were being watched,
Was undismayed, and so I went along.
We came to terms. I had my travelers' checks,
And he had bills of large denominations
Rolled into wads, stuffed in his jacket pockets.
He mockingly let me examine one.
It seemed genuine enough. I agreed to exchange
Two hundred dollars' worth of travelers' checks.
He counted out the bills before my eyes,
Folded them neatly into a thick packet,
And I in turn carefully signed my checks,
And we made our exchange. And then he smiled
A smile of condescension and insolence,
Waved to me with a well-manicured hand
On which he wore a number of gold rings

And disappeared. Throughout this both of us
Knew we had been intensively observed
By the two thugs who stood across the square.
They must have seen the large bulge in my pocket
And I was now certainly too mistrustful
To count the bills once more in sight of them
Or ask of them the way to my hotel.
So I made the return home by trial and error,
And only within the confines of my room
Did I discover that my wad of bills
Was almost wholly folded newspaper.
At first, of course, I was furious; Martha thought me
A gullible fool, which didn't improve my mood.
Two hundred dollars is not a trifling sum,
But after a while I began to realize
That Ercole's fine clothes were the pathetic
Costume and *bella figura* of the poor.
For him, like other Neapolitan sinners,
Staying alive, the sheer act of survival,
Was a game of cunning I was quite unused to
And involved paying off confederates:
The helpless urchin outside our hotel,
The two thuggish observers, whose mere presence
Had kept me from discovering the fraud
Until too late, and may have distracted me
(I pride myself on being a keen observer)
From the skilled legerdemain of those adept,
Tapered, manicured, bejewelled hands.

I I I

See, what a perfect day. It's perhaps three
In the afternoon, if one may judge by the light.
Windless and tranquil, with enough small clouds
To seem like innocent, grazing flocks of heaven.

The air is bright with a thickness of its own,
Enveloping the cool and perfect land,
Where earthly flocks wander and graze at peace
And men converse at ease beside a road
Leading to towers, to battlements and hills,
As a farmer guides his cattle through a maze
Of the chipped and broken headstones of the dead.
All this, serene and lovely as it is,
Serves as mere background to Bellini's painting
Of *The Transfiguration.* Five dazzled apostles,
Three as if just awakening from sleep,
Surround a Christ whose eyes seem to be fixed
On something just behind and above our heads,
Invisible unless we turned, and then
The mystery would indeed still be behind us.
A rear-view mirror might perhaps reveal
Something we cannot see, outside the picture
But yet implied by all Bellini's art.
Whatever it is seems to be understood
By the two erect apostles, one being Peter,
The other possibly John, both of them holding
Fragments of scroll with Hebrew lettering,
Which they appear just to have been consulting.
Their lowered eyes indicate that, unseeing,
They have seen everything, have understood
The entire course of human history,
The meaning and the burden of the lives
Of Samson, Jonah, and Melchizedek,
Isaiah's and Zechariah's prophecies,
The ordinance of destiny, the flow
And tide of providential purposes.
All hope, all life, all effort has assembled
And taken human shape in the one figure
There in the midst of them this afternoon.
And what event could be more luminous?
His birth had been at night, and at his death
The skies would darken, graves give up their dead.

But here, between, was a day so glorious
As to explain and even justify
All human misery and suffering.
Or so, at least, perhaps, the artist felt,
And so we feel, gazing upon a world
From which all pain has cleanly been expunged
By a pastoral hand, moving in synchronous
Obedience to a clear and pastoral eye.
    By this time, having gazed upon as much
Painting in the *Museo Nazionale*
As could reasonably be taken in
On a single morning, we make our way outside
Only to be confronted by the *pompe*
Funebri of six jet-black harnessed chargers,
Each with black ostrich plumes upon his head,
Drawing a carriage-hearse, also beplumed,
Black but glass-walled, and bearing a black coffin
Piled with disorderly hot-house profusions
Of lilies, gladioli, and carnations.
The sidewalk throngs all cross themselves, and Martha
Seems especially and mysteriously upset
In ways I fail to understand until
Back in our room she breaks out angrily:
"Didn't you see how small the coffin was?"
I am bewildered by this accusation.
Of course I *saw*, but thought it far more prudent
To leave the topic delicately untouched.
I am annoyed at her and at myself,
An irritation I must not let damage
What yet remains of this holiday of ours.

IV

Two days of rain. Confining. Maddening.
From our French windows and our small *balcon*
We watch the cold, unchanging, snake-skinned bay

Curtained by leaden sheets of rain in which
Capri and Procida are set adrift
Beyond the limits of sight, like the *Wandering Isles.*
We are housebound, quarantined. We read and fret,
Trying our best to be cheerful and good humored,
And it occurs to me that only a nation
Devoted to the cult of the Madonna
With all its doctrinal embellishments
Could produce "extra-virgin olive oil."
Martha is not amused by this; the rain
Has damped her spirits, and she has been reading
Grand-guignol sections on Tiberius
In Seutonius' gossipy old book.
The weather itself feels like those steel engravings
Of the *Inferno* by Gustave Doré:
A ruthless, colorless, unvarying gray.
So that when sunshine comes we are astonished,
Filled both with gratitude and with amazement
At the brilliant flowers in the public squares.
We elect to spend the morning simply sunning
In the great park of the *Villa Nazionale,*
And find ourselves almost restored to normal
When we become reluctant witnesses
To a straggling parade of freaks and mutants
From a local hospital for the handicapped
On a brief outing to the aquarium.
They are extraordinary: stunted, maimed,
Thalidomide deformities, small, fingerless,
Mild pigmentless albinos, shepherded
Into a squeaky file by earnest nuns
Between the sunlit bushes of azaleas.
They seem like raw material for the painting
Of Bosch's *Temptation of St. Anthony:*
Wild creatures, partly human, but with claws
Or camel humps, or shrivelled, meager heads.
What they will see inside those glassy tanks
(Thick sullen eels, pale sea-anemones)

Will be no odder than what they are themselves.
Martha, who never ventures anywhere
Without me, and has not a word of Italian,
Has disappeared.
                    I am deeply alarmed.
It suddenly seemed that she might be the victim
Of some barbaric or unthinkable crime:
That, kidnapped, she was being held for ransom,
Or worse. I hurried back to the hotel,
And found her, deeply shaken, in our room,
Unwilling to talk, unwilling, at first, to listen
To any attempt to soothe or comfort her.
I tried to tell her in what must have been
A way that somehow frightened or offended
That life required us to steel ourselves
To the all-too-sad calamities of others,
The brute, inexplicable inequities,
To form for ourselves a carapace of sorts,
A self-preservative petrific toughness.
At this she raised her arm, shielding her eyes
As if she thought I were about to strike her,
And said *No* several times, not as a statement,
But rather as a groan. And then she gave me
A look the like of which I can't describe.
I left her in possession of the room
And spent the rest of the day pacing the lobby,
Taking my tea alone. She finally joined me
For a dinner at which not a word was uttered
On either side.
                    What struck me during the meal
(As if confirming everything I'd told her)
Was a vivid recollection from that morning:
Not of the warped and crippled, but of the reds,
Among the pale profusions of azaleas,
The brilliant reds of the geraniums.

V

Somewhere along in here, deeply depressed,
I ceased making journal entries, so what follows
Is pretty much an uncertain reconstruction
Concerning our brief excursion to the baths
Of Nero and the surrounding countryside.
It was intended as a light diversion
Into the realms of luxury and ease,
A little apolaustic interval.
Were we wrong, I wonder, to expect so much?
I looked at the map, and saw the *Mare Morto,*
And innocently thought of the Holy Land.
We entrusted ourselves meekly to the hands
Of a guide (found for us by our concierge),
An older man of dignified appearance
Who spoke fair English and was named Raimondo.
His smile was reassuring; we were both
Impressed and pleased by his enthusiasm.
Baiae was once a fashionable resort.
Caesar and Nero and Caligula
Had built their summer villas on this coast.
But Nero's baths were desultory ruins,
Tangled in chicory and acanthus growth,
Littered by tourists, and excrement of dogs.
The hills around are honey-combed with caves,
And Raimondo told us with naive excitement
Of the Sibyl's Cave, the old worldly-wise Sibyl
Who cunningly foxed and outwitted Tarquin,
Obliging him to buy her three last books
For the full price of nine by coolly burning
A set of volumes each time he refused.
But first Raimondo had another cave
Picked for our delectation: damp and foul-smelling,
It was, of course, the well-known *Grotta del Cane,*

Known in the ancient texts as *Charon's Cave.*
The brimstone odors here rise from a depth
No one can measure, keeping the very earth
Throughout this region perpetually warm—
So much that when Raimondo cut some turf
With a penknife and handed me a clod
I could feel heat from subterranean fires.
It's to these bottomless thermal wells of warmth
That all this region owes its opulence,
Its endless summer *wo die Zitronen blühn.*
A man and a mongrel now enter the cave,
Answering Raimondo's summons. We are to view
The ghastly and traditional death-scene.
But only after the no less traditional
And ceremonious haggling about fees,
A routine out of *commedia del'arte.*
And then, by the scruff of the neck, the master forces
His dog's head close to a rank and steaming fissure
Where fumes rise from the earth, the stink of Dis,
That place of perfect hospitality
"Whose ancient door stands open night and day."
The dog's eyes widen in unseeing terror;
It yelps feebly, goes into wild convulsions,
And then falls limp with every semblance of
Death. Being then removed and laid
Near the cave's mouth, in about thirty seconds
It starts to twitch and drool, then shakes itself,
And presently staggers to its four feet.
With a broad wink and conspiratorial smile,
Raimondo says that by modest computation
That dog dies three hundred times a year,
And has been earning its own livelihood
As well as its owner's for about three years.
This puts it well ahead of Lazarus,
Orpheus, and the others who have made
Sensational returns. As the Sibyl said
Solemnly to Aeneas, "The way down

Is easy from Avernus—but getting back
Requires a certain amount of toil and trouble."
Avernus, as it happens, the stinking lake
No bird can fly across, all birds avoid,
Lies within easy access, as does the Cave
Of Cumaean Sibyl, both of which Raimondo
Encourages us to visit, but we insist
That we have had enough of caves and smells
To last us for a while, so he proposes
A little tour of the Elysian Fields,
The region of the blurred and blissful dead.
Virgil has made it seem a lovely place,
A heroes' health-club, a gymnasium
Of track-stars, wrestlers, athletes, all engaged
In friendly contest, sun-tanned rivalry.
Here, too, convened all those distinguished ghosts
Who had bettered life by finding out new truths,
Inventing melodies or making verses,
At home in a faultless landscape of green meadows
Watered by streams of dazzling clarity.
What we saw was something different. There was, of course,
No fabulous descent to a nether world.
Instead Raimondo took us to a place
Where, we assumed, he meant to let us pause
Before some planned approach to the sublime.
But he said to us, quite lamely, "This is it.
This is the place called the Elysian Fields."
(I checked his claim that evening in the guide-book,
And the map proved that he had told the truth.)
It was a vacant wilderness of weeds,
Thistles and mulberries, with here and there
Poplars, quite shadeless; thick, ramshackle patches
Of thorny amaranth, tousled by vines.
This wild, ungoverned growth, this worthless, thick,
And unsuppressible fecundity
Was dotted with a scattering of graves
Of the most modest sort: worn, simple stones

From which all carving had been long effaced,
And under which the mute, anonymous dead
Slept in supreme indifference to the green
Havoc about them, the discourse of guides,
The bewildered tourists, acres of desolation.

VI

Marriages come to grief in many ways.
Our own was, I suppose, a common one,
Without dramatics, a slow stiffening
Of all the little signs of tenderness,
Significant silences, self-conscious efforts
To be civil even when we were alone.
The cause may be too deep ever to find,
And I have long since ceased all inquiry.
It seems to me in fact that Martha and I
Were somehow victims of a nameless blight
And dark interior illness. We were both
Decent and well-intentioned, capable
Of love and devotion and all the rest of it,
Had it not been for what in other ages
Might have been thought of as the wrath of God,
The cold, envenoming spirit of Despair,
Turning what was the nectar of the world
To ashes in our mouths. We were the cursed
To whom it seemed no joy was possible,
The spiritually warped and handicapped.
It seems, in retrospect, as I look over
The pages of this journal, that the moments
Of what had once seemed love were an illusion,
The agreement, upon instinct, of two people
Grandly to overestimate each other,
An accord essentially self-flattering,
The paradise of fools before the fall.

A LOVE FOR FOUR VOICES
Homage to Franz Joseph Haydn

For Frank and Ruth Glazer

FIRST VIOLIN	HERMIA
SECOND VIOLIN	HELENA
VIOLA	LYSANDER
CELLO	DEMETRIUS

I *Allegro Moderato*

HERMIA

Here we have fallen transposingly in love,
And the fireflies, the Japanese lanterns, flare
With little conjugate passions, images of
The cordial, chambered ignitions of the heart.
Far down below, the lilting, debonair
Pleasure craft blink and wander in the cove
Like slippery constellations, as if man's art
Had made a prayer rug of the firmament,
A broad-loomed duplicate night wherein to trace
Patterns of happy prospect, drawn from the blent,
Breath-taking features of a cherished face.

Lemon verbena blooms in the tufa wall,
And the mild night air, warm as our whispered words,
Circulates like a bloodstream, invisible
Yet parallel as smooth ascending thirds
To our most inward workings. Warmth and youth,
All the clear promptings of this clement weather,
Invest our bodies with a looming truth
To be pursued and husbanded together.

LYSANDER

Playing along the fringe of this delight
    Slides a strange warning finger,
Not hers, not mine, not the blind god of love's
    (To whom we serve as braille)
But yet indicative of another night
    Prepared as though with cloves
In the fixed future, where neither glance shall linger
    Nor pulse nor god prevail.

Diminished sevenths, modular descents
    Full of alarming jumps
And sudden accidentals strike a note,
    Brief as a lovers' quarrel,
That shakes us with an obscure significance.
    Like a whiff of creosote
Tainting the garden, they proclaim in trumps
    The *carpe noctem* moral.

These dissonances but serve to underscore
    The score nobody knows
Except the taciturn composer, Fate.
    Sensing at the deep base
Of our being the ultimate cadences before
    They gather to their close,
We feel the fickle fingering and confess
    It's already getting late.

HELENA

You think you know who you are, when all at once
          You stand amazed:
Love has pulled off one of its major stunts,
And the routine view in the mirror now displays
Merits unrecognized in other days.
          The weather's clear and fine,
Or, if it's raining, everything is glazed,
          Becrystalled and benign.

But who's that nymph the cheval glass now discloses?
          This calls for thought.
It seems to you you've seen her. Couched on roses?
Attended by a little, wingèd brood?
Somewhere. Perhaps in Kenneth Clark's "The Nude,"
          Bearing the alias
Of *Miss O'Murphy*, or superbly wrought
          In ravishing undress

By Renoir or Correggio or Lachaise.
          All this is due
To the interest and the steady, upright ways
Of a lad who seems the third, or efficient, cause
Of a sort of constant ringing of applause
          Or oceanic roar
Mounting in acclamations just for you
          From the whole Atlantic shore.

And then you know: you are the latest find
          Of Hollywood
Featured in private screenings of the mind
In an inventory of post-Freudian sex
Called "Civilization and its Discothèques."
          In a lingua franca phrase
Of body language at last you've understood
          What gauds and gilds your days.

DEMETRIUS

Mine is the firm bass clef that shall unlock
A world of passions in our *théâtre à clef*
Which is all about the ways of human clay
When freed from the simple props of summer stock.

Enter, Myself, for a turn about the stage.
I muse on the causes of my ecstasy,
Displayed well-stacked in billowing deshabille,
Yielding in levantine concubinage.

Yet I am nothing if not cynical.
Wherein does she delight me save in this:
That I indorse upon her with a kiss
A mound attaining to some pinnacle,

That there's no feature of me but promotes
Her insatiety, that I adore
Merely my lonely self as, more and more,
I am the singular thing on which she dotes.

I am Narcissus, she simply the pool,
Obliging, selfless, bright, wherein I see
Intoxicating images of Me,
Classical, isolate, withdrawn and cool.

TUTTI

Now, in a highly sharpened signature,
We sign away our lives for the duration,
And each of us, determined on seduction,
Makes his insinuating overture.
Organ involuntaries, crotchet songs,
Bed chamber measures, operatic lays,
Each goes its cunning, predetermined ways,
Seeking the counterpart for which it longs.

Time's of the essence, and will not permit
Eight hands, eight legs, two staffs and one joint purpose
Any returning, any starting over,
Nor can the ingenuities of wit
Alter the text or term of this our opus
That binds in ligatures beloved and lover.

I I *Minuetto: Presto ma non troppo*

LYSANDER

Question: Isn't to fall in love to fall
Away from Time or out of it, to break
Tempo in a sort of contretemps,
Flouting the linear ways of chronicle?
Only in fantasies and tales of love
Can we imagine the "terminally well."

HELENA

Agreed, my dear. Love is in fact the nostrum,
Compounded of plain meum/tuum simples,
That takes its crabbed critic by the throat
And renders him a tender Juvenal.

HERMIA

Lovers and tourists enjoy the luxury
Of being set apart from daily life.
Morning refinishes Saint Polycarp
With aureate platings, sunny encrustations,
And beneath a café awning the tourist savors
Chicory-coffee fumes as a profligate fountain
Casts up before his eyes whole velvet trays
Of cabochons and brilliants. Yet what absorbs him
Are the small transformations, the differences
That invest the simplest fixtures of the world.
Windows and telephones, coins and umbrellas,
Are all, as it were, recast in foreign terms.

DEMETRIUS

And so it is, as you were going to say,
With lovers. They pass through familiar sordors,
Worn curbstones foul with uncollected garbage,
Which they translate into the Côte d'Azur.
Noting the gleam on the lip of a coffee mug,
They remember all the ricochets of light
That return from darkened corners in Vermeer,
Reflective, upon a beautiful young servant.

TUTTI

Love comes like capers to the Aurelian Wall,
Capricious, goat-like, ready to undermine
The whole imperial enterprise, and split
With little wedging tentacles and roots
The masonry of the Tabularium.
Spring and the goddess prompt these penetrations
And intimate subversions. They revive
Grape hyacinth and crocus and raise up
Daily with promise long-standing hopes and members.
Anadyomene, restless, of the waters,
Powerful, rash and salty, hear our prayer.
Make glad our passage with your ritornello;
Furnish each humble thing that greets our sight
With pure ipseity; transpose the world
With augmentations of your major theme.

I I I *Andante: post coitum triste*

DEMETRIUS

Late afternoon. The canted light
Sieves down through elevated glooms
Of linden, sycamore and beech
As lengthening shadows stripe the grass.
The cricket concertmaster's A
Is taken up through the dense fields,
Heavy with scent and irony,
Dotted with common everlasting,
Bitter dock and cocklebur.
From the cool shadows of this rock,
These crowding blues and heliotropes,
As from some attic of my youth
I gaze out at the distances
That contrast renders almost white,
Like frocks of garden-party girls
I once knew or desired to know,
Speckled and flecked by shadow-leaves
Like missing jigsaw puzzle parts.
And whether the girls were known or not,
Whether those yearnings were stillborn
Or were met with kindness, now they lie
Like quilts of sunlight spread to dry,
Scattered and thin and dimly gold
And permanently out of reach—
Small flags of failure, or, at best,
Triumphs with all their glory lost.
Between post oak and propter oak
Falls the inevitable shade.

HERMIA

Out of the cotton batting clouds, the scentless gauze
    Of sleep, out of the pendulous rockabye
Of dreamt treetops, one floats down leaf-like to be
       received
    Without resistance by the sustaining bed
As, one by one, the faculties grab their discarded
    Clothing and make themselves decent, the five
Little senses answer the rollcall roster of school
    And that ten o'clock scholar, the mind, late
As always, shows up confused, asking, "Where am I?"
    Nothing's familiar. The chiffonière, majestic
In seasoned tones of briar, the tall, lead-weighted drapes
    Declare that overnight and all unmerited
You have risen in the world. And curiosity
    On just that point calls you to the window seat
At what you suppose to be the bedlington gray of pre-
       dawn.
    It's not. A long drizzle has brought the worms
To their flagstone deaths, and across the barbered lawn a
       soaked
    Flag hangs limp on its epicene pole. Neither breeze
Nor birdsong, but the drainpipe from the gutters overhead
    Rattles its tinny chimes or liquid vocables.
Near at hand stone urns of the balustrade darken with
       charcoal
    Weathering, and far away the trees take umbrage
In the disconsolations of the mist. And then it all comes
       back.
    You turn as if for confirmation, and there it lies,
Fred Trismegistus himself, sleeping the Sleep of the Just
    Plumb Tuckered Out, rapt in some dream of which he
Is the much-cheered, totally adored hero of stadiums
    Full of nubile, half-clad girls, in which he
Is the sole male, the halfback, half-baked, sexy medalist
    Who lolls in insolent Iotacism,

Giving himself up gratefully to that famous first
    Infirmity of an ignoble mind. About
Two, perhaps, he may so much come to himself as to
    Discover that what he really needs is a
Bath and a shave. But meanwhile your own clothes, strewn
        here and
    There, begin to recall your imbecilities
Of last night. What will your hostess, a friend since grade
        school, say?
    Better get dressed as quietly as possible
And slip out for a cold, long, sobering walk.

HELENA

Take Waller's stoic, gladiatorial rose,
Saluting you as it prepares to die
On orders, simply to make a vulgar point:
That Time and the poet's nose are out of joint,
That flesh is grass, and he's a blade who grows
Green till he has what you can best supply.

But for pure instruction nothing can compare
With those gigantic, momentary blooms
In the sequined colors of a two-bit whore:
Metallic-blue chrysanthemums that soar
Over our heads and homes, dangle in air,
Decline and blacken to their instant dooms

Quicker than you can say "Jack Robinson."
The question is: what are they telling us?
If life is brief, that sex is even briefer,
Its joys like the illusions of a reefer
Decaying from the moment they're begun
And scarcely worthy of such struggle and fuss?

LYSANDER

Man, that with the heated imagination of a poet lies down in the finest linens to caresses, must rise in due course *from the sack* in all the frosty solitude of a philosopher. "How came this spell upon me," he inquires, "that made my very flesh to stand on end? made me, who am otherwise all head, vision and mind, become mere fundament, pure Bottom, someone's ass?" It is sheer fantasy confers such powers: I vote her beautiful out of my need. Her grace is in the gland of the be- holder. This is plain masturbation, thinly disguised, in which I dub her my sea-born Galatea, and she brightly replies, "Baby, you're aces." Bodies themselves in plain truth are no more shapely than potatoes; they are as pallid of flesh and take up their residence under the same brown sod. Let him who can be aroused by a potato plight his true oath and purchase wedding bands. I, divested of illusions, must now inhabit among essences.

I V *Finale: vivace assai*

HELENA

What prompts the ichor of the gods
    To race along their limbs?
Young, well-developed human bods,
    Succulent hers and hims.
Shamelessly these divine ones flirt
    With those of mortal race,
And, one may add, it doesn't hurt
    Having a comely face.

LYSANDER

In divers incarnations they,
    As bull or swain or swan,
Devote themselves to carnal play
    And wildly carry on,
And gotten up in festal guise
    Or bestial masquerade
Contrive to get themselves lengthwise
    Definitively laid.

HERMIA

No quarry can elude their quest
    Or can divert the mind
Of those who batten on a breast
    Or well-defined behind.
Theirs is a gleeful *vie de bohème*
    Unbound by moral codes
In which they work the lawless claim
    Of virgin mother-lodes.

49

DEMETRIUS

Like smoothly polished Phidian nudes
    Of vast and sculptured shape,
They cast themselves in attitudes
    Of statutory rape.
Vigorous their pursuit of bliss,
    Emphatic and *tout court*,
From which no earthly orifice
    Is perfectly secure.

TUTTI

And shall not humble humankind
    Aspire to godly ways,
Utter the disembodied mind
    In fleshly paraphrase?
Therefore come all ye neophytes,
    Observe the Rule of Thumb;
With ever more intense delights
    And mounting pleasures, come!

HERMIA

It has been left to me now to supply
The modest coda, close and epilogue
Of this machineless masque, beg your indulgence
For all our author's incapacities,
And crave your pardon if he has offended.
The loves we have enacted, the sweet neumes
And melodies played out in artful casts
Of baited lines and characters, were not
Mere casual rousings of the rampant id.
They exhibit a certain play, free, natural,
Yet harmonious charmingly, as if our lives,
As you would like to hope, had a design
Not to be seen here in the thick of things.
But the thick of things is not beside the point.
The gray felt daylong dusk of winter skies,
The golden, noontide braveries of midsummer,
Odors of harvest apples, the cursive lines
Of one known hand, pressed clover leaves between
The India paper leaves of Second Kings,
A voice, the expectation of a voice,
Quavers of light and semibreves of joy
Confirm the only magic of the world
Here where we fall transposingly in love.

IV

ANTHEM

These birds pursue their errands
    On curvatures of air;
Like swift and lyric gerunds
    Unfurling everywhere,
They lash the sky with ribbons,
    With wakes of wrinkled blue,
Chanting Orlando Gibbons
    And Mozart's *Non so più.*

Shall we not in all conscience
    And glittering major keys
Offer them fair responsions
    And reciprocities?
Fanfares and sound fulfillings
    Of melodies unheard:
Brave philharmonious Billings
    And airs of William Byrd.

ANTAPODOSIS

For Mona and Jarvis

I

You send us your used weather, the gray serge
Of clouds, hand-me-down rain that has picked up
Its acid comment in transit through Ohio,
Second-hand blizzards, wrinkled isobars
That thunder eastward in an aerial surf.
Stuff the Salvation Army wouldn't touch!
Soiled, threadbare, obsolete, your record lows
Low like lost herds of Angus, like bull markets
Among the shivered stocks and bonds of heaven,
The china shop of stars, come blundering in
And let us have it, and of which we plain
In plaintive plainsong and the plainest terms
That the Great Plains and Hoagy Carmichael
Provided: "You've Come a Long Way From St. Louis."

II

We send you our used daylight, mildewed dawns,
Rusted sunset finales that have seen
Better days, wasted afternoons as stale,
Flat and unprofitable as *The New York Sun,*
Drypoint editions of New England dusk,
Ghostly crepuscules straight from the photo morgue.
Shrunk by inflation, our diminished savings
Of late November light, like little hairless
Chihuahuas, seem doll-house versions of the Dog Days.
And finally, the soft night having arrived,
Scented with sweetgrass, garrulous with crickets,
The sky Columbian Blue, you lift your eyes,
And what do we hand you but "The Great White Way,"
Our name in lights, somewhat the worse for where.

HUMORESQUE

*Passengers will please refrain
from flushing toilets while the train
is standing in the station. I love you.*

From sewage lines, man-holes, from fitted brass
Sphincters and piston chambers, from the dark
Gastro-intestinal corridors of hell,
Deep among wheels and oily underbellies
Of *Wagon Lits* emerge these screeching ghosts,
Doomed for a certain term to walk the night,
Erupting here and there in baggy forms
That cloud, occlude and spirit away the luggage,
Facteurs and passengers from this vast barn
Of skeletal iron and grimed membranes of glass.
This pestilent congregation of vapors sings
In Pentecostal tongues, now shrill, now soft,
Mixed choral dolorosos by Satie
To the god Terminus, the living end
Of every journey, whom the Romans charmed
With gifts of blood and ashes, and who today
Comes up from under as pale S. Lazare,
Come back to tell us all, and tell us off,
And tell and tell, as the bells toll and trains
Roll slowly to their sidings, issuing ghosts.
These rise and fade into the winter air
Already gray with souls of the departed
Through which indifferent pigeons lift and bank
And flutter in the vague and failing warmth,
Which, like the curling lamias of *Gauloises,*
The shiny rigor mortis of the rails,
Blends with the exhalations of my love.

NAMING THE ANIMALS

Having commanded Adam to bestow
Names upon all the creatures, God withdrew
To empyrean palaces of blue
That warm and windless morning long ago,
And seemed to take no notice of the vexed
Look on the young man's face as he took thought
Of all the miracles the Lord had wrought,
Now to be labelled, dubbed, yclept, indexed.

Before an addled mind and puddled brow,
The feathered nation and the finny prey
Passed by; there went biped and quadruped.
Adam looked forth with bottomless dismay
Into the tragic eyes of his first cow,
And shyly ventured, "Thou shalt be called 'Fred.'"

ENVOI

A voice that seems to come from outer space,
Small, Japanese, (perhaps the pilot of
One of these frisbee saucer flights that trace
Piss-elegant trajectories above

Sharp eyes and index finger landing pads)
Speaks to me only with its one-watt tweeter
(A dodderer among these dancing lads)
And firmly orders: "Take me to your reader."

My Muse. I'd know her anywhere. It's true
I'm no Bob Dylan, but I've more than one
Electric fan who likes the things I do:
Putting some English on the words I've spun

And sent careening over stands of birch
To beat the local birds at their own game
Of taking off and coasting in to perch,
Even, perhaps, in pigeon-cotes of fame.

They are my chosen envoys to the vast
Black Forests of Orion and The Bear,
Posterity's faint echo of its past,
And payload lifted into haloed air.

A BOUNTIFUL HARVEST

The Rev. Elisha Fawcett, . . a Man-
chester Evangelist, . . devoted his life
to teaching the natives of the Admi-
ralty Islands the Commandments of
God and the Laws of Cricket. Too
poor to purchase a monument to this
good man, his parishioners erected
his wooden leg upon his grave. In
that fertile clime it miraculously took
root and for many years provided a
bountiful harvest of bats.

As if mistaking a foghorn for The Last Trump,
This risen limb, come forth before its time,
Dryadic, out of a turned and varnished stump,
A Lazarus with one foot still in the grave

(To whom some shameless newsman presses his query,
"What was it like . . . I mean . . . *you know* . . . down there?"
And with all the sad reserve of the truly weary,
The leaves signal their dignified "No Comment"),

This umbrageous Evangelical Christmas tree
Is festooned with a troupe of gymnasts all in gray
Instead of with globes and tinsel, a filigree
Of bats, or acrobats, hung upside-down

As if to receive a well-timed fling of wrists
Or ankles, and known as "The Flying Pipistrelli."
Their capes wrapped close about them, these aerialists
Let their blood pool in their tiny frontal lobes

And dream they are now, in the words of the secular Pope,
"The light *Militia* of the lower Sky,"
Attendant Sprites, cruising through stroboscope,
Slow-motion frames of inner loops and dives,

Guided by sonar wit or the saintly folly
Of those the World at large describe as "batty,"
Raising their little, high-pitched, melancholy
Squeaks in a Chapel hymn by Isaac Watts.

The Commands of God and Ordinances of Cricket
Meshed and were married in the good man's sermon
Titled, "The Straight Gate is a Sticky Wicket,"
Still quoted with approval at church picnics,

And all the parish point with ordinate praise
To the leafy witness of the life that died
And rose again in green (with some scattered grays.)
That went forth, was fruitful, and multiplied.

V

CROWS IN WINTER

Here's a meeting
of morticians in our trees.
They agree in klaxon voices:
things are looking good.
The snowfields signify
a landscape of clean skulls,
Seas of Tranquility
throughout the neighborhood.

Here's a mined,
a graven wisdom,
a bituminous air.
The first cosmetic pinks
of dawn amuse them greatly.

They foresee the expansion of graveyards,
they talk real estate.
Cras, they say,
repeating a rumor
among the whitened branches.

And the wind, a voiceless thorn,
goes over the details,
making a soft promise
to take our breath away.

IN MEMORY OF DAVID KALSTONE

who died of AIDS

Lime-and-mint mayonnaise and salsa verde
Accompanied poached fish that Helen made
For you and J.M. when you came to see us
Just at the salmon season. Now a shade,

A faint blurred absence who before had been
Funny, intelligent, kindness itself,
You leave behind, beside the shock of death,
Three of the finest books upon my shelf.

"Men die from time to time," said Rosalind,
"But not," she said, "for love." A lot she knew!
From the green world of Africa the plague
Wiped out the Forest of Arden, the whole crew

Of innocents, of which, poor generous ghost,
You were among the liveliest. Your friend
Scattered upon the calm Venetian tides
Your sifted ashes so they might descend

Even to the bottom of the monstrous world
Or lap at marble steps and pass below
The little bridges, whirl and eddy through
A liquified Palazzo Barbaro.

That mirrored splendor briefly entertains
Your passing as the whole edifice trembles
Within the waters of the Grand Canal,
And writhes and twists, wrinkles and reassembles.

POEM WITHOUT ANYBODY

In memory of James Wright

Mid-ocean. Nightfall. No one. The sea spray
Is spattered upward out of a dark body
As if determined to become air, and falls,
A failure, back to its laced and slippery troughs,
Its sliding, undulant gulleys of polished black.
The winds battle each other, the ravelled air
Tumbles across cold miles of desolation,
Plunging and spilling over a punished surface.
Here are no grandeurs and no sufferings,
Neither the grim particulars of wrongs
Nor hope nor courage. Here all the doubtful postures
Of history, pride, and language fall away.
The surge continues its untiring violence,
The foam of outrage, Promethean helplessness,
Bound fast to its own mindless element.

Dear Jim, I call to you across the darkness
Where we are emptied of all our vanities,
Where none of our pleas is answered. Beyond the slosh
And wet, beyond the salt tumulous puzzle,
Beyond millions of deaths, loss and injustice,
The derelict shacks, the bare neglected farms,
May it please these muscular powers to rehearse
Your pain and whispered words, lavish their tears
On all the waste of which you are the image,
And by their own tormented energy
To be lifted out of themselves, a floating mist,
Gray, neutral, passionless, and modified,
A delicate shawl of sorrow, lingering
Into horizonless indifference,
The cold, blank rock-face of a sunless day.

TO L. E. SISSMAN, 1928–1976

Now "a spring breath of Lux across the Charles"
Salutes the freshman noses that detect
On trellises of the laboring intellect
Faint emblematic blooms of Vaughan and Quarles

Along with poisonous minerals and exhausts
Of Donne and Ford and Kissinger and Chevy.
The Yard is green, and sophomores note the heavy
Strokes on the metered tennis courts of Frost's

Athletic quatrains: this *ars* which endures
Beyond the *vita brevis* will bother heads
Of bra-less, liberated, cool co-eds
For many a spring to come, craft such as yours,

Dear friend, whose poetry of Brooklyn flats
And poker sharps broadcasts the tin pan truths
Of all our yesterdays, speaks to our youths
In praise of both Wallers, Edmund and Fats,

And will be ringing in some distant ear
When the Mod-est, last immodesty fatigues,
All Happenings have happened, the Little Leagues
Of Pop and pop-fly poets disappear

To join, with all their perishable lines,
The Edsel, Frug, beau monde of Buzzard's Gulch,
The wisdom and the wit of Raquel Welch,
"And connoisseurs of California wines."

THE TRANSPARENT MAN

I'm mighty glad to see you, Mrs. Curtis,
And thank you very kindly for this visit—
Especially now when all the others here
Are having holiday visitors, and I feel
A little conspicuous and in the way.
It's mainly because of Thanksgiving. All these mothers
And wives and husbands gaze at me soulfully
And feel they should break up their box of chocolates
For a donation, or hand me a chunk of fruitcake.
What they don't understand and never guess
Is that it's better for me without a family;
It's a great blessing. Though I mean no harm.
And as for visitors, why, I have you,
All cheerful, brisk and punctual every Sunday,
Like church, even if the aisles smell of phenol.
And you always bring even better gifts than any
On your book-trolley. Though they mean only good,
Families can become a sort of burden.
I've only got my father, and he won't come,
Poor man, because it would be too much for him.
And for me, too, so it's best the way it is.
He knows, you see, that I will predecease him,
Which is hard enough. It would take a callous man
To come and stand around and watch me failing.
(Now don't you fuss; we both know the plain facts.)
But for him it's even harder. He loved my mother.
They say she looked like me; I suppose she may have.
Or rather, as I grew older I came to look
More and more like she must one time have looked,
And so the prospect for my father now
Of losing me is like having to lose her twice.
I know he frets about me. Dr. Frazer
Tells me he phones in every single day,
Hoping that things will take a turn for the better.
But with leukemia things don't improve.

It's like a sort of blizzard in the bloodstream,
A deep, severe, unseasonable winter,
Burying everything. The white blood cells
Multiply crazily and storm around,
Out of control. The chemotherapy
Hasn't helped much, and it makes my hair fall out.
I know I look a sight, but I don't care.
I care about fewer things; I'm more selective.
It's got so I can't even bring myself
To read through any of your books these days.
It's partly weariness, and partly the fact
That I seem not to care much about the endings,
How things work out, or whether they even do.
What I do instead is sit here by this window
And look out at the trees across the way.
You wouldn't think that was much, but let me tell you,
It keeps me quite intent and occupied.
Now all the leaves are down, you can see the spare,
Delicate structures of the sycamores,
The fine articulation of the beeches.
I have sat here for days studying them,
And I have only just begun to see
What it is that they resemble. One by one,
They stand there like magnificent enlargements
Of the vascular system of the human brain.
I see them there like huge discarnate minds,
Lost in their meditative silences.
The trunks, branches and twigs compose the vessels
That feed and nourish vast immortal thoughts.
So I've assigned them names. There, near the path,
Is the great brain of Beethoven, and Kepler
Haunts the wide spaces of that mountain ash.
This view, you see, has become my Hall of Fame.
It came to me one day when I remembered
Mary Beth Finley who used to play with me
When we were girls. One year her parents gave her
A birthday toy called "The Transparent Man."

It was made of plastic, with different colored organs,
And the circulatory system all mapped out
In rivers of red and blue. She'd asked me over
And the two of us would sit and study him
Together, and do a powerful lot of giggling.
I figure he's most likely the only man
Either of us would ever get to know
Intimately, because Mary Beth became
A Sister of Mercy when she was old enough.
She must be thirty-one; she was a year
Older than I, and about four inches taller.
I used to envy both those advantages
Back in those days. Anyway, I was struck
Right from the start by the sea-weed intricacy,
The fine-haired, silken-threaded filiations
That wove, like Belgian lace, throughout the head.
But this last week it seems I have found myself
Looking beyond, or through, individual trees
At the dense, clustered woodland just behind them,
Where those great, nameless crowds patiently stand.
It's become a sort of complex, ultimate puzzle
And keeps me fascinated. My eyes are twenty-twenty,
Or used to be, but of course I can't unravel
The tousled snarl of intersecting limbs,
That mackled, cinder grayness. It's a riddle
Beyond the eye's solution. Impenetrable.
If there is order in all that anarchy
Of granite mezzotint, that wilderness,
It takes a better eye than mine to see it.
It set me on to wondering how to deal
With such a thickness of particulars,
Deal with it faithfully, you understand,
Without blurring the issue. Of course I know
That within a month the sleeving snows will come
With cold, selective emphases, with massings
And arbitrary contrasts, rendering things
Deceptively simple, thickening the twigs

To frosty veins, bestowing epaulets
And decorations on every birch and aspen.
And the eye, self-satisfied, will be misled,
Thinking the puzzle solved, supposing at last
It can look forth and comprehend the world.
That's when you have to really watch yourself.
So I hope that you won't think me plain ungrateful
For not selecting one of your fine books,
And I take it very kindly that you came
And sat here and let me rattle on this way.

THE BOOK OF YOLEK

Wir haben ein Gesetz,
Und nach dem Gesetz soll er sterben.

The dowsed coals fume and hiss after your meal
Of grilled brook trout, and you saunter off for a walk
Down the fern trail, it doesn't matter where to,
Just so you're weeks and worlds away from home,
And among midsummer hills have set up camp
In the deep bronze glories of declining day.

You remember, peacefully, an earlier day
In childhood, remember a quite specific meal:
A corn roast and bonfire in summer camp.
That summer you got lost on a Nature Walk;
More than you dared admit, you thought of home;
No one else knows where the mind wanders to.

The fifth of August, 1942.
It was morning and very hot. It was the day
They came at dawn with rifles to The Home
For Jewish Children, cutting short the meal
Of bread and soup, lining them up to walk
In close formation off to a special camp.

How often you have thought about that camp,
As though in some strange way you were driven to,
And about the children, and how they were made to walk,
Yolek who had bad lungs, who wasn't a day
Over five years old, commanded to leave his meal
And shamble between armed guards to his long home.

We're approaching August again. It will drive home
The regulation torments of that camp
Yolek was sent to, his small, unfinished meal,
The electric fences, the numeral tattoo,
The quite extraordinary heat of the day
They all were forced to take that terrible walk.

Whether on a silent, solitary walk
Or among crowds, far off or safe at home,
You will remember, helplessly, that day,
And the smell of smoke, and the loudspeakers of the camp.
Wherever you are, Yolek will be there, too.
His unuttered name will interrupt your meal.

Prepare to receive him in your home some day.
Though they killed him in the camp they sent him to,
He will walk in as you're sitting down to a meal.

MURMUR

Look in thy heart and write. SIDNEY

O heart, O troubled heart— YEATS

A little sibilance, as of dry leaves,
Or dim, sibylline whisper, not quite heard:
Thus famously the powers that be converse
Just out of earshot, and theirs is the last word.
Officiously they mutter about our lives.
The die is cast, they say. *For better or worse.*

Thus the Joint Chiefs. Thus, too, the Underground.
Soft susurrations reach us where we repose
On a porch at evening. We notice a vague uproar
Of bees in the hollyhocks. Does the darkening rose
Hum with an almost imperceptible sound?
That small vibrato, is it news of a distant war?

You've seen the night nurse, who hugs your fever chart
Defensively to her bosom's alpine slopes,
Confer with an intern who lounges against a wall,
A boy not half your age. They converse apart.
And nothing they say seems to provoke a smile
As they stand there earnestly trifling with your hopes.

And remember again the long-distance telephone
When you're asked to hold the line, and way far off
A woman's cracked-voiced, broken-hearted plea
Is answered only by a toneless cough.
You have stumbled upon some gross fatality
There in the void—quite possibly your own.

This latest leak from an invisible source
Speaks like the slave appointed to hover near
The emperor, triumph-crowned in gold and myrtle,
And regularly to breathe in Caesar's ear
As they pursue the *via sacra's* course
Through the great crowds, "Remember you are mortal."

A Note About the Author

ANTHONY HECHT's first book of poems, *A Summoning of Stones*, appeared in 1954. He is also the author of *The Hard Hours*, which won the Pulitzer Prize for poetry in 1968, of *Millions of Strange Shadows*, 1977, and of *The Venetian Vespers*, 1979. He is the translator (with Helen Bacon) of Aeschylus' *Seven Against Thebes*, 1973, and coeditor (with John Hollander) in 1967 of a volume of light verse, *Jiggery-Pokery*. A collection of his critical essays, *Obbligati*, was published in 1986. He has received the Bollingen Prize in Poetry, the Librex-Guggenheim Eugenio Montale Award and is presently University Professor in the Graduate School of Georgetown University.

A Note on the Type

The text of this book was set in a typeface called
WALBAUM, named for Justus Erich Walbaum (1768–
1839), a typefounder who removed from his beginnings in
Goslar to Weimar in 1803. It is likely that he produced this
famous type face shortly thereafter, following the designs of
the French typefounder, Firmin Didot. His original matrices
are still in existence, owned by the Berthold foundry of Ber-
lin. Continuously popular in Germany since its inception,
the face was introduced to England by the Monotype Cor-
poration in 1934, and has steadily grown in popularity ever
since.

Composition by Graphic Composition, Inc., Athens, Georgia
Printed and bound by Halliday Lithographers, West Hanover, Massachusetts
Designed by Harry Ford